Great Coin Tricks

Bruce Smith

Sterling Publishing Co., Inc.
New York

Editor: Shona Grimbley
Consultant Magicians: Anthony Owen and Marc Paul
Designer: Graham Curd at wda
Illustrator: Colin Woodman

**Library of Congress Cataloging in Publication Data
Available**

10 9 8 7 6 5 4 3 2 1

Published by Sterling Publishing Company, Inc.
387 Park Avenue South New York, NY 10016
First Published in Great Britain
under the title *Coin and Banknote Tricks*
© 1995 Arcturus Publishing Limited/ Bruce Smith
Distributed in Canada by Sterling Publishing
c/o Canada Manda Group, One Atlantic Ave, Suite
105, Toronto, Ontario, Canada M6K 3

Manufactured in the United States of America
All rights reserved

ISBN 0-8069-7177-0

Contents

Simple Stuff	4
Basic Sleight-of-Hand Vanishes	13
Productions	24
Penetrations	47
Feature items	73
Advanced Coin and Banknote Tricks	79
The Basics	80
Transposition	95
Clever Stuff	100
Advanced Productions	108
Advanced Penetrations	118
Feature Effects	143
Index	159

SIMPLE STUFF

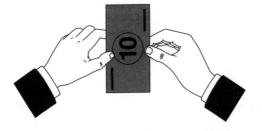

JUMPING COIN

Effect *A coin vanishes from the magician's right hand to appear in the left.*

Requirements *Any two coins.*

Preparation *None.*

• • • • • • • • • • • • • • • •

1 Show a coin on the palm of each hand (illustration 1). The coin in the left hand should be below the third and fourth fingers. The one in the right hand should be at the base of the thumb. Hold the hands 30cm/12in apart on a table top.

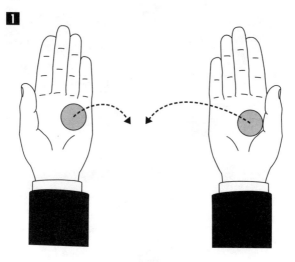

2 At exactly the same time turn both hands over quickly so that the thumbs come close together. As you do this the coin from the right hand will be thrown under the left hand (illustration 2), but to the audience it appears that you have just turned your hands over and there is a coin under each one.

3 Lift your right hand to show that the coin has vanished. Lift the left hand to show that amazingly there are now two coins under it.

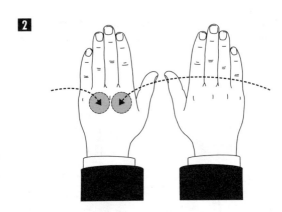

TOP TIPS FOR TRICKSTERS

Money magic is always more effective if the coins or banknotes used in the trick are borrowed from trustworthy members of the audience.

REFLEX TESTER

Effect *This is not a magic trick, but a stunt or "scam" you can try on your friends, using a banknote, to prove that there is no such thing as "easy money". If you use their money perhaps you can make a profit!*

Requirements *Any banknote.*

Preparation *None.*

● ● ● ● ● ● ● ● ● ● ● ● ● ● ● ●

1 The right thumb and first finger hold a note vertically at the middle of the right long edge. The open left hand is in position at the middle of the left long edge, but the left hand must not touch the note (illustration 1).

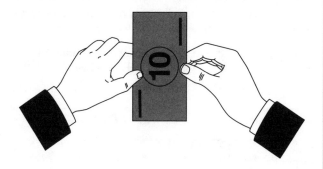

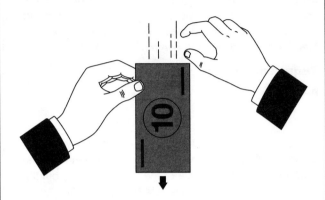

2 The right hand releases the note and the left hand instantly closes to catch it (illustration 2). You can repeat this a few times to show your "punter" how easy this is.

3 Now ask your friend to hold his open left hand at the center point of the left long side – the position your left hand was in a moment ago.

TOP TIPS FOR TRICKSTERS

Tricks with coins are fine for showing a few people close up, but – with a few exceptions (like the "Miser's Dream") – are not really suitable on stage.

4 Tell them that if they catch the bill they can keep it!

5 Let go of the bill with your right hand and watch it slip through your friend's fingers to the floor (illustration 3).

Although this looks easy, nobody will be fast enough to catch the money.

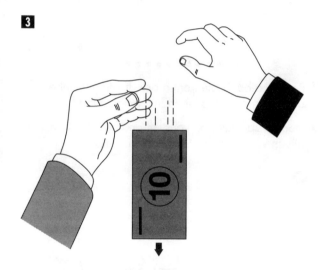

TOP TIPS FOR TRICKSTERS

If you do perform coin productions on a stage it is worth while having the coins silver plated so that they will shine in the stage lights and be easier to see.

VANISHING NOTE

Effect *A banknote is borrowed and rolled up into a tight tube. When it is handed to a member of the audience the note vanishes. It reappears in the magician's pocket.*

Requirements *A banknote (which you borrow from a member of the audience).*

Preparation *None.*

• • • • • • • • • • • • • • • •

1 Borrow a banknote from a rich, trusting member of your audience and roll it up into a tight tube.

2 Stand a spectator on your left and hold the banknote tightly in your right hand to stop it unrolling.

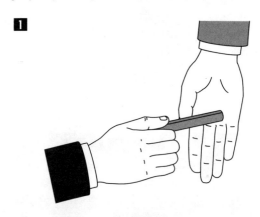

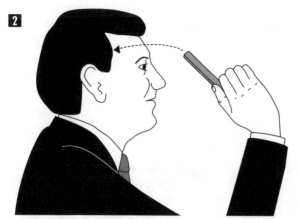

3 Ask the spectator to hold out their right hand palm up. With your left hand hold on to their right wrist.

4 Lift the note up and bring it down to tap the spectator's open hand (illustration 1). Explain that on the count of three the spectator must close their hand around the note.

5 Swing your right hand up in an arc to the right of your face (illustration 2) and back down. Count "one" as the note taps their open hand. Repeat this action and count "two" as you tap their palm again.

6 The next time your hand swings up, you leave the rolled up note tucked behind your ear. The timing must be the same as before – the right hand swings back down as though nothing has happened.

7 Your extended first finger hits the spectator's hand. The spectator will instinctively close their hand around your finger. Ask them to open their hand so that you can have your finger back! This creates an amusing situation for a few moments when it seems that the money has vanished inside the spectator's hand.

8 You can either reveal that the note is tucked behind your right ear or have a duplicate note in your pocket which you can return to your money lender.

The effect makes a great bar bet and stunt, and can be used as a gag or as a strong piece of magic. However, it is not really suitable for a stage presentation.

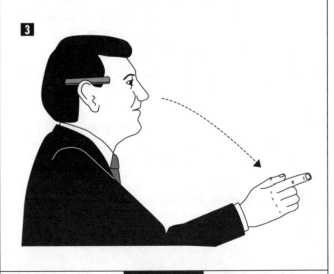

BASIC SLEIGHT-OF-HAND VANISHES

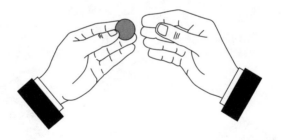

THE FINGER PALM VANISH

Effect *A coin vanishes.*

Requirements *Any coin.*

Preparation *None.*

● ● ● ● ● ● ● ● ● ● ● ● ● ● ● ●

1 Display the coin lying at the base of your right fingers.

2 Rest the edge of your right little finger across your left fingers (illustration 1).

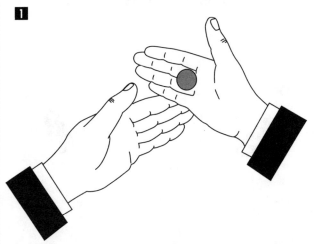

3 Pivot the right hand inward towards you, apparently

2

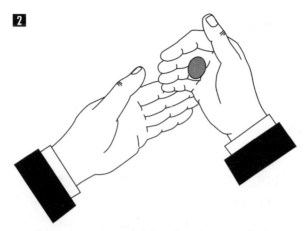

to tip the coin into your left hand. In fact your right fingers curl inwards to hold the coin securely in the right fingers. This is the finger palm position (illustration 2).

4 Your left hand closes as though it did contain the coin. It moves downwards and turns over, drawing the audience's attention to it. Point with the right hand and move the left hand away to the left (illustration 3).
5 You can now casually lower your right hand to your

TOP TIPS FOR TRICKSTERS

If you are performing any coin tricks remember that the audience's attention will be on your hands. Ensure that you give them a good wash before you perform!

side as attention is on the left hand. Slip the coin into your right pocket or keep it finger-palmed to be reproduced later.

6 Slowly open the left hand to show the coin has vanished.

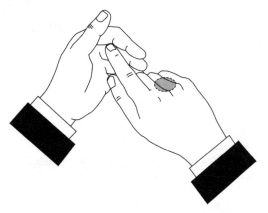

TOP TIPS FOR TRICKSTERS

Before you perform any tricks that will involve the audience concentrating on your hands make sure that you have clean fingernails!

THE FRENCH DROP

Effect *A coin vanishes.*

Requirements *Any coin.*

Preparation *None.*

• • • • • • • • • • • • • • •

1 Hold the coin horizontally, parallel with the floor, with the tips of your left thumb and fingers. The fingers and thumb should be pointing upwards. Your fingers should be held together so that nobody can see between them.

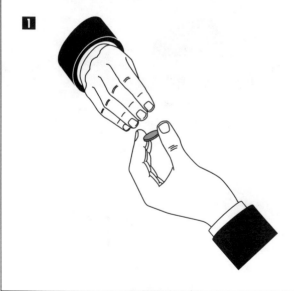

2 Your right hand approaches from behind to apparently pick up the coin (illustration 1). Your right thumb goes under the coin and your right fingers come over the top.

3 As soon as your right fingers cover the coin from view your left thumb releases the coin, allowing it to fall to the base of your left fingers (illustration 2).

4 However, your right hand continues as though it did contain the coin. It clenches into a fist and moves upwards and away to the right (illustration 3). It is important that you watch the right hand move and hold

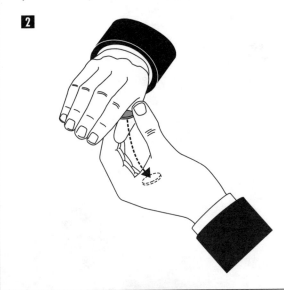

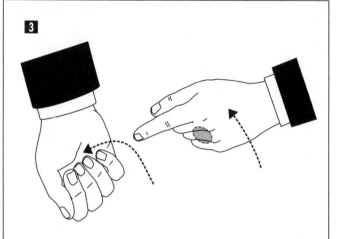

the left hand still. The rules of misdirection to remember here are first, that the audience will watch a moving object, and second, they will look where you look.

5 Close the left hand, clipping the coin at the base of the left fingers (finger palm position).

6 Open your right hand to show that the coin has vanished!

TOP TIPS FOR TRICKSTERS

It is worth while washing your hands before and after you practice as coins can become grubby and dirty very easily.

🪙 THE PINCH VANISH 🪙

Effect *A coin vanishes in the magician's hands.*

Requirements *Any coin.*

Preparation *None.*

• • • • • • • • • • • • • • • •

1 Hold the coin vertically in your left hand, at the tips of your thumb and first three fingers (illustration 1). Keep your fingers tight together so that the audience cannot see between them. The backs of your fingers are towards the audience.

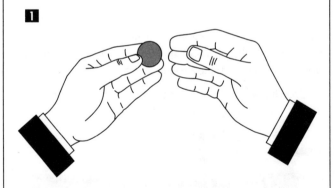

2 The right hand reaches over as though to take the coin from the left hand. The right thumb goes behind the coin and the right fingers cover it at the front.

2

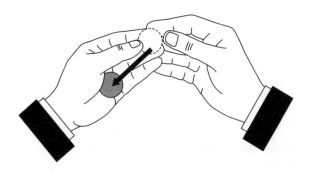

3 As soon as the right fingers completely cover the coin from the audience's view the left thumb releases its hold, and the coin slides down to the base of the left fingers (illustration 2).

DAVID ROTH

This New York coin magician is probably today's acknowledged expert at sleight-of-hand magic with coins. Many of his routines are described in detail in the book, David Roth's Expert Coin Magic, *written, illustrated and published by Richard Kaufman and available from most good magic shops.*

4 The left hand curls slightly to hold the coin in the finger palm position while the right hand moves away to the right, apparently taking the coin (illustration 3).

5 Watch your moving right hand, and allow your left hand to drop naturally to your side. Keep the backs of the right fingers towards the audience so that they do not know the coin is not there (illustration 4).

6 While attention is on your right hand you can secretly slip the coin into your left pocket or keep it finger palmed to be reproduced later.

7 Slowly open the fingers of your right hand to show the coin has vanished!

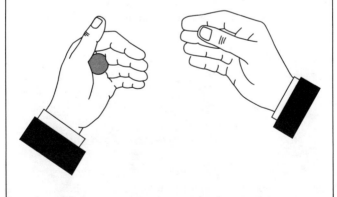

4

CHUNG LING SOO (1861-1918)

One of the highlights of Chung Ling Soo's spectacular show was the "Dream of Wealth". From mid-air he produced coins, banknotes and a check for one million dollars! Although known as the Marvellous Chinese Conjurer, the Asian character was actually a disguise for William E. Robinson who was really born in America! He was fatally wounded on stage during a performance of the famous "Catching a Bullet,"

PRODUCTIONS

MONEY MAKING MACHINE

Effect *The magician shows a banknote, folds it into a tube and tips out a genuine coin!*

Requirements *Any banknote and coin.*

Preparation *Place the coin and banknote in your pocket so that they can easily be removed together.*

• • • • • • • • • • • • • • •

1 Reach into your pocket and remove the banknote and coin, ensuring that the coin is kept concealed behind the note. Explain to the audience that this is your private Money Making Machine!

2 Hold up the note with the right hand, holding the hidden coin clipped to the back of the note with the right thumb (illustration 1).

3 Snap the left side of the note with the left fingers. This proves to the audience that the left hand is empty and that nothing is concealed behind the left side of the banknote.

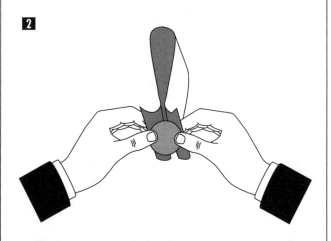

2

TOP TIPS FOR TRICKSTERS

Gimmicked and fake coins will enable you to do many more tricks – but it is essential to master the basics of sleight-of-hand magic first.

3

4 Hold the left side of the note in the left hand mirroring the right hand's grip. Bring the two hands together making the note bend as in illustration 2. Secretly transfer the coin from under the right thumb to under the left thumb. Flick the right side of the bill with the right first finger (illustration 3).

PAUL DANIELS (b. 1938)

Paul Daniels is Britain's best known magician, due to his many series of The Paul Daniels Magic Show *on BBC1 and his live performances in theaters around the country. One of his most memorable television performances was the day he made £1,000,000 cash vanish – and reappear! Watching over him on that occasion was newspaper tycoon Robert Maxwell!*

4

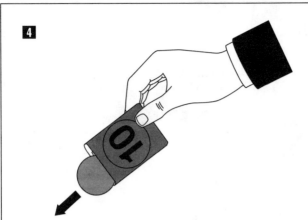

5 Fold the note into a tube, secretly wrapping the concealed coin inside.

6 Tilt the opening in the folded note downwards so that the coin slowly falls out (illustration 4). You have proved that you have made your own Money Making Machine!

FRED KAPS (1926-1980)

This Dutch magician was a master of sleight of hand and manipulation. He was a winner of many famous magical awards – a true World Champion. His act featured the manipulation of banknotes and giant coins, and concluded with the production of an almost endless stream of salt pouring from his fist.

MULTIPLY YOUR MONEY

Effect *The magician displays at his fingertips a coin of small denomination (for example, a penny). With a magical pass the magician changes it into two coins, both of a much higher value than the original coin!*

Requirements *Three coins (one small and two large).*

Preparation *The two large coins are held upright near the tips of your right thumb and first finger. They are secretly hidden by the smaller coin which you hold upright and at right angles to them, also at the tips of the right thumb and first finger (illustration 1). Hold this set-up in front of a mirror and you will see that the two*

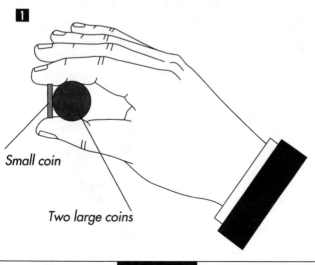

Small coin

Two large coins

large coins are hidden. Practice the following routine many times in front of a mirror watching it from different angles until you are confident the large coins are completely hidden.

Set up the coins in position and you are ready to begin your performance.

• • • • • • • • • • • • • • • •

1 Hold up the right hand to show the small coin face on and at the audience's eye level so that they cannot see the two extra coins (illustration 2). The trick will only work if the coin is held at the height of the audience's line of vision. It is important that the edges of the large coins are at the exact center of the small coin, to give as much cover as possible.

2

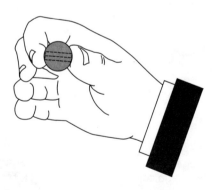

3

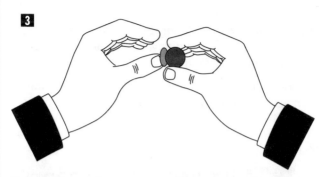

2 The audience have, apparently, seen that your right hand is empty, except for the small coin. Now show both sides of your left hand to prove it is empty.

3 Bring the two hands together with the first fingers and thumbs of both hands pointing towards each other. Again it is essential that the hands stay level with the audience's eye level so they do not see the extra coins.

4 Your left thumb goes beneath the coins, pushing on the bottom edge of the small coin (illustration 3), pivoting it on to the bottom of the two large coins so that all three coins are now in one stack.

TOP TIPS FOR TRICKSTERS

It is a good idea to keep a set of coins especially for performing with. Keep these polished and clean to improve your "professional" image.

5 At the same time tip the three coins forward so that the top coin of the pile (a large coin) faces the spectators head on. The small coin is now hidden at the back of the coin stack (illustration 4).

6 Move your two hands apart; the left hand takes the front coin to the left and the right hand holds the other two coins clipped together and moves them to the right. The small coin is now concealed behind the large coin in the right hand, and held in place by the right thumb.

It will seem that the small coin has grown and doubled in an instant. As you put the coins away be careful not to expose the small hidden coin.

This is a quick visual effect which is ideal for a one-to-one performance, especially when creating extra change at the shop, bank or on the bus!

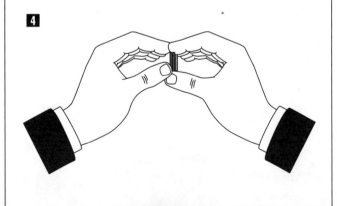

CONTINUOUS COINS

Effect *The magician borrows a handkerchief from a spectator and produces an apparently endless stream of coins from within its folds.*

Requirements *A large cotton handkerchief (preferably borrowed from a member of the audience) and two identical coins – the larger the better.*

Preparation *Place one coin in your left trouser pocket and one in your right trouser pocket. You are all set to produce money from nothing!*

● ● ● ● ● ● ● ● ● ● ● ● ● ● ●

1 Borrow the handkerchief and show it on both sides. Show both your hands are empty so there is no suspicion of you sneaking anything into the handkerchief.

2 Point the fingers and thumb of your right hand upwards with all the tips touching. Your left hand drapes the handkerchief over your right hand so that the pointed fingers are in the center of the handkerchief.

3 Show your left hand is empty and, with the left hand, grasp the center of the handkerchief and lift it up. You are going to exchange the positions of your hands so that your left hand is under the handkerchief and your right hand is uncovered. Flip the handkerchief with your right hand and throw it over the left hand. The left hand takes position with the fingers pointing up (illustration 1).

3

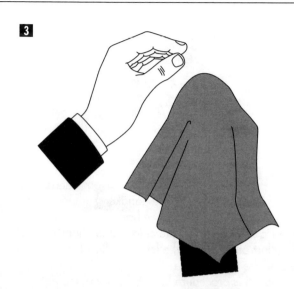

4 You say that you can see something sticking out of the top of the handkerchief, apparently held by the left fingertips. With your right hand you mime taking the object, keeping the back of the hand towards the audience so they cannot see if you have taken anything or not.

5 Place the right hand in your righthand pocket, apparently to dispose of the object. In fact you finger palm the coin in your pocket. The audience's impression should be that you are putting something in your pocket, *not* secretly removing something!

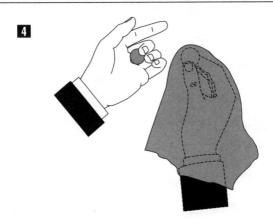

4

6 Your right hand grasps the center of the handkerchief again (illustration 2) and the left hand flips the handkerchief over the right hand, reversing the positions. Throughout this procedure keep the back of the right hand towards the audience so that the concealed coin remains hidden.

7 Again pretend there is an object in the center of the handkerchief and mime taking it with the left hand (illustration 3). Your left hand goes to the left pocket to apparently dispose of the object. In fact it finger palms the coin there and reappears with the coin concealed.

8 The left fingers take hold of the center of the handkerchief – and, through the material, of the coin in the right hand. The coin in the left hand remains hidden in the finger palm position (illustration 4).

9 The now empty right hand flips the handkerchief back over the left hand as described in step 3. But this time you reveal that a coin has magically appeared in the center of the handkerchief (illustration 5)!

10 Take the coin in your right hand and place it in your right pocket. In your pocket slide the coin back into the finger palm position and remove the apparently empty right hand. It will appear that you have deposited the coin in your pocket.

11 Now the right hand grasps the center of the handkerchief – and the coin which was finger palmed in the left hand. The left hand flips over the handkerchief to show another coin has appeared (illustration 6)!

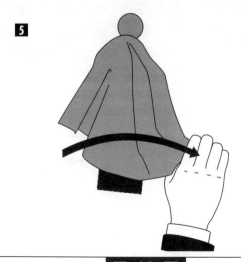

5

12 The left hand takes the coin and places it in the left pocket where you slide it back into finger palm!

13 By repeating steps 8 through to 12 you can produce an apparently endless stream of coins from within the folds of the handkerchief – just by reproducing the same two coins.

When you think you have profited enough, return the handkerchief to its owner and take your applause.

There is plenty of potential for humor with this effect as you pretend that the owner has got a coin trapped in the folds of their handkerchief. . . and another. . . and another. . . which you keep pocketing until you return the handkerchief!

🪙 MISER'S DREAM 🪙

Effect *This is one of the true classics of coin magic, performed by professional magicians all over the world. The magician plucks coins from the air and drops them into a container. In the finale the magician's hands are full of a stream of gleaming coins caught in mid-air.*

Requirements *A special fake coin, a stack of genuine identical coins (about 25), a container (a large tin or a small plastic bucket) and a special holder.*

Preparation *The special coin is made by drilling a hole in a small metal disc the same size as the coins (a blank pet's name tag is ideal for this as it already has*

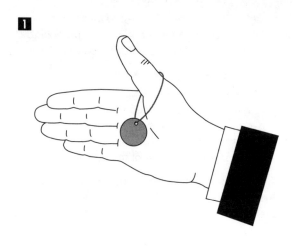

the hole in it). Thread a small loop of cotton through the hole so that it will loop over your thumb (illustration 1).

The special holder is made from an old sock! This will hold the stack of coins that will make your big final production (about 12). To make the holder cut off the toe of the sock and sew around the edge of the hole with elastic (illustration 2). Put half the coins inside the sock – the elastic should prevent them falling out – and safety pin it under your jacket or coat on your right side.

Your final preparation is to loop the thread on the fake coin over your right thumb and stack the remaining coins (about 12) in your closed left hand. The empty container should be on your table.

All this set-up means that it is best to perform the "Miser's Dream" as an opening effect. It is particularly suitable for this because it is short and noisy!.

● ● ● ● ● ● ● ● ● ● ● ● ● ● ● ●

1 Pick up the container with the right hand and show the audience that it is empty (keeping the special coin hidden in your hand). Pass the container to your left hand which takes it, holding the coins between the left fingers and the inside top edge of the container.

2 Reach forward with the right hand apparently to pluck a coin from the air. Keep the back of the fingers towards the audience to hide the coin dangling from your thumb. Jerk your hand upwards and the coin will flip up to your fingertips – apparently produced in mid-air.

2

3 Move the right hand to the top of the container and apparently drop the coin inside. What really happens is that you release the coin and it returns to its position dangling around the thumb. At the same time your left fingers allow one coin inside the container to drop to the bottom – the audience will hear it drop. If the timing is right this is very convincing – it seems as though you have just dropped a coin into the container.

TOP TIPS FOR TRICKSTERS

Many fake and gimmicked coins are available from magic shops, dealers and suppliers. You may find a magic shop listed in your local Yellow Pages.

4 By repeating step 2 you can apparently produce another coin! Repeat step 3 and drop it into the container.

3

TOP TIPS FOR TRICKSTERS

You can have great fun with money magic at any time. When out shopping you can produce the correct change from mid-air or vanish a note as you hand it to the bank cashier!

5 Continue producing coins until all the coins in your left hand have been dropped into the container. You can produce coins from behind your knee, under your armpit or from your audience! It is a very funny situation to apparently produce coins from behind a spectator's ears, or beard and so on.

6 When the last coin has been dropped, allow your right hand to fall naturally to your side as you shake the container noisily and perhaps jokingly ask if anyone would like to contribute to your collection! While the audience's attention is on the container, your right hand reaches under the right side of your jacket and squeezes the coins out of the holder. Any noise made while you're doing this will be covered by you rattling the container in your left hand.

7 Finally place the container on the table or the floor and open your right hand, letting the final big production of coins stream from your hand into the container (illustration 3). The special coin will fall unnoticed among the regular coins.

STREET MAGICIANS

Many magicians began their performing lives "on the street" as buskers, trying to extract money from the passers-by. Ex-street magicians enjoying great success today include Harry Anderson, John Lenahan, Keith Fields, Leo Ward and Penn and Teller.

ALTERNATIVE APPEARANCE

Effect *This is an alternative way of producing the single coin in your right hand when you are performing the "Miser's Dream." It uses a regular coin.*

Requirements *Any coin.*

Preparation *None.*

• • • • • • • • • • • • • • • •

1 The coin begins in the "thumb clip" position (illustration 1). The coin is clipped between the base of the right thumb and the first finger. The coin is hidden from the audience as throughout the routine the back of the right hand faces the audience.

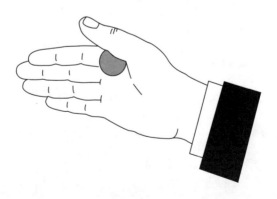

2

2 The four right fingers all bend inwards (illustration 2). The first finger goes behind the coin and the second finger in front as they clip the coin.

3 To produce the coin the fingers open out again, the first and second fingers bringing the coin into view clipped between them (illustration 3).

TOP TIPS FOR TRICKSTERS

The most important thing in coin magic is to make your hand look natural when it is secretly concealing a coin. If your hand looks tense and cramped it will be noticed. The best advice is to keep a coin "palmed" in your hand all day so that you forget about it – it will help you to act more naturally during a performance.

3

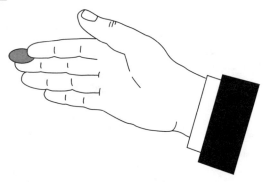

4 To apparently drop the coin into the container simply reverse the procedure. As the right hand moves over to the container, the right fingers close and the right thumb clips the coin again. The right fingers can now be spread and shown to be empty. The coin can then be produced again. . . and again. . . and again.

AL GOSHMAN (1921-1991)

New York magician Al Goshman was one of the first and finest close-up magicians. Until his death he was one of the resident magicians at the Magic Castle in Hollywood. Throughout his act, if you said "please," he would produce a successsion of coins from beneath a salt cellar – each coin bigger than the last.

PENETRATIONS

COIN UP THROUGH HAND

Effect *The magician places a coin in the left fist. When he slaps the back of the fist with his right hand the coin appears on top of his fist, having apparently penetrated his hand!*

Requirements *Any coin.*

Preparation *None.*

● ● ● ● ● ● ● ● ● ● ● ● ● ● ● ●

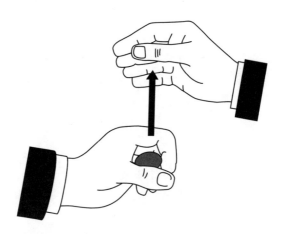

2

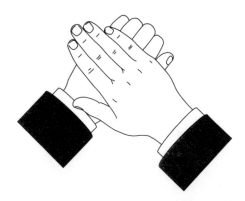

This is a quick visual stunt which looks like clever sleight of hand, but relies more on a special knack which will only take a few minutes to learn. It is not suitable for a big show, but it is fun to do for a few friends with a borrowed coin.

1 Place the coin in your left hand. Close the hand around it in a loose fist, turned palm down.

2 You now appear to simply slap the back of the left hand with the right. As you do this, jerk both hands up slightly and release the coin from the left fist (illustration 1).

3 The coin will fly out of the left fist, hit the right palm and land on the back of the left hand. The right hand then slaps the back of the left, holding the coin in place (illustration 2).

4 Lift the right hand off the left fist to show that the coin has apparently penetrated the hand and landed on the back of the left hand (illustration 3).

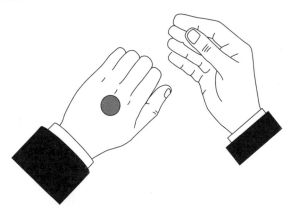

PROFESSOR HOFFMANN (1839-1919)

Professor Hoffmann was the pen-name of Angelo Lewis, a professional barrister and journalist, who was Britain's leading magical author. The first coin tricks to be described in detail appeared in his books. His books are now rarities, sought by magical collectors everywhere. His books included Modern Magic, More Magic, Later Magic *and* Magical Titbits.

COIN THROUGH LEG

Effect *The magician passes a borrowed coin through his right leg!*

Requirements *Any coin (preferably borrowed) and a right leg that is wearing trousers!*

Preparation *None.*

• • • • • • • • • • • • • • •

1 Borrow a coin from a member of your audience. If they wish they can mark it with a pen or crayon.

2 Hold the coin between the right thumb and fingers.

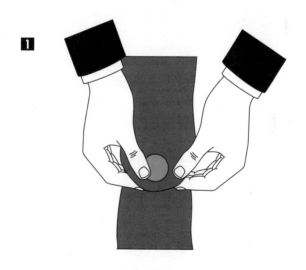

2

3 Place the coin on your right leg just above the knee. The right thumb holds the coin against your trouser leg.

4 With the fingers of both the left and right hands fold a piece of material of the trousers up and under the coin (illustration 1).

5 Fold the material you have pulled under the coin up and over to cover the coin (illustration 2). The left thumb holds the fold of material in position.

6 When the coin is completely covered by the material the thumb of your right hand secretly pulls the coin up into the right hand behind the right fingers (illustration 3).

7 Your right hand now curls slightly to finger palm the coin. Move your right hand around to the back of the right leg. The left fingers keep hold of the fold of trouser material which is apparently trapping the coin.

8 Release your left hand's grip on the material. It will drop, revealing that the coin has gone. Turn your left hand around to show that it is empty.

9 With your right hand, remove the coin from behind the right knee by pushing the coin from the finger palm position up to the fingertips. It appears that the coin passed through your leg!

This is a great trick for an impromptu performance for just a few people.

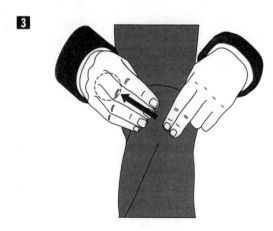

COIN ESCAPE

Effect The magician gives a spectator seven coins to hold. Despite the fact that the spectator holds the coins tightly inside their fist, the magician makes one coin penetrate through the spectator's hand.

Requirements Seven coins of identical value.

Preparation None.

• • • • • • • • • • • • • • • •

1 Hold the coins in your cupped left hand and stand facing the spectator who is going to assist you.

2 Ask the spectator to hold out their hand palm up ready to receive the coins.

3 With your right hand pick up the first coin and place it in the spectator's hand counting "one" (illustration 1). Continue to count the next four coins, allowing each one to click against a coin already in their hand – this gets

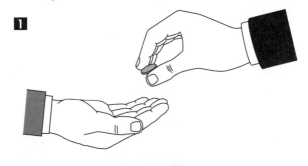

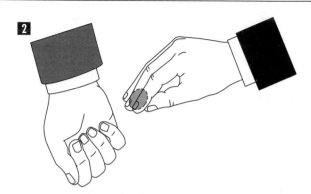

them used to hearing the coin go into their hand. This will allow you to "short change" them in the next step.

4 When you place the sixth coin in the spectator's hand simply click it against a coin already in their hand, but do not let go of it. Keep it gripped between the right thumb and first finger. Make sure that the coin remains concealed by your right fingers.

5 Throw the final coin from your left hand straight into the spectator's right hand. They will snap their fist closed (illustration 2).

6 Bring your right hand underneath their fist, keeping the coin concealed. Slap your hand against the back of their fist. Slide your hand out from underneath revealing a coin in your fingers. Ask them to open their hand and count the coins. One coin has magically penetrated through their hand!

PENETRATING NOTE

Effect *Two notes of different denominations are placed on the table, one on top of the other. Magically they penetrate through each other.*

Requirements *Any two banknotes (preferably borrowed). The only requirement is that they must be of different values or currency so that they can be told apart.*

Preparation *None.*

• • • • • • • • • • • • • • • •

1 Lay the two notes on the table to form a V. The point of the V is towards you. The lower note is angled away

2

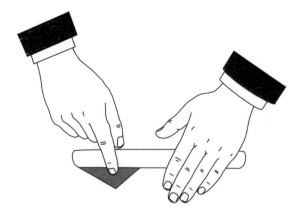

to your left and the upper note angled away to your right. It is important that the note on top is slightly further forward toward the audience. It does not quite meet the edges of the lower note.

2 Make sure the audience is clear which note is on top.

3 Beginning at the point of the V use your two first fingers to start rolling the notes together (illustration 1).

4 Continue rolling until only a small part of a corner of the lower note is visible on the table. When you reach this point stop rolling. More of the upper note will be sticking out as it began slightly further forward.

3

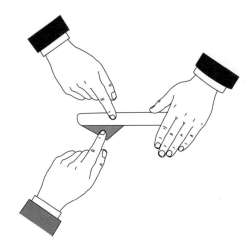

5 Cover the visible corner of the lower note with your left hand. Do this while your right finger points to the corner of the upper note sticking out on the right (illustration 2). Ask a spectator to place a finger on the corner on your right (illustration 3).

6 As they do this, secretly roll the notes forward slightly. Under cover of your left hand, the left corner will flip around the roll – it will go under the rolled up notes and flip back on to the table in its original position. This is the secret move which makes the trick work.

7 Lift your left hand and ask the spectator to place a finger from their other hand on that corner.

8 Point out to the audience that the corners of both notes are now being pinned to the table. Explain this makes any trickery impossible – unknown to them it has already happened!

9 Unroll the notes towards you and show that – incredibly – the two notes have passed through each other. The note that was on top is now below (illustration 4).

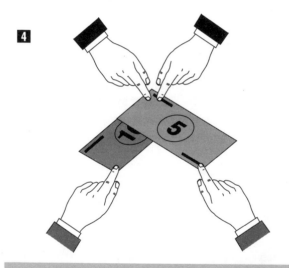

TOP TIPS FOR TRICKSTERS
With a few well practiced coin tricks which you can perform with any coins you will always be able to entertain friends any time, any place, anywhere!

CRASH GLASS

Effect A borrowed coin penetrates through the bottom of a glass tumbler, ending up trapped inside.

Requirements Any coin (the heavier the better) and a smooth-sided glass tumbler. It is more effective if these are both borrowed. This is a great trick to do in a bar or at the dinner table with an empty glass that is sitting nearby.

Preparation None.

• • • • • • • • • • • • • • • •

1 Hold the glass in the left hand gripped by the thumb and little finger, with the mouth of the glass against the

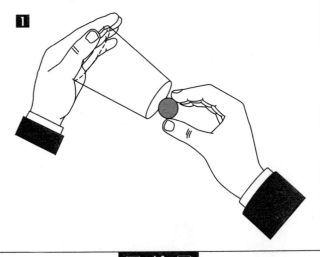

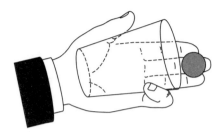

left palm. It is important that the other fingers can be moved without disturbing the grip on the glass.

2 Display the coin in the right hand. Hold it with the right fingertips and tap it against the bottom of the glass (illustration 1).

3 Part the hands and quickly bring them back together. As your hands come back together the coin is released by the right hand and, moving with the momentum provided by the right hand, travels in front of the glass and is caught by the extended left fingers (illustration 2).

TOP TIPS FOR TRICKSTERS

Money magic is not particularly suitable for an audience of young children as they may not be familiar with currency or its value.

3

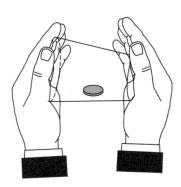

4 As soon as the left hand catches the coin it moves to the left, then jerks back to the right causing the coin to fly inside the glass. At the same time the right hand slaps against the bottom of the glass (illustration 3).

5 Because the coin travels too fast for the eye to follow, it appears to the audience that the coin has visibly penetrated through the bottom of the glass.

PENN AND TELLER

This outrageous American duo have shocked audiences around the world with their "sick tricks" and upset many magicians. They began their performing careers as street entertainers and are now in demand for TV shows and live performances – and have even made their own movie – Penn and Teller Get Killed.

MYSTERY OF THE SEALED BOX

Effect *An empty matchbox is shown and placed in the center of the table. The magician places a coin under the table. The coin vanishes from under the table and can be heard appearing inside the closed matchbox!*

Requirements *A regular matchbox and two identical coins.*

Preparation *Slide one of the coins between the bottom of the tray and the outer cover. Close the matchbox, keeping the coin concealed in its hiding place (illustration 1).*

• • • • • • • • • • • • • • • •

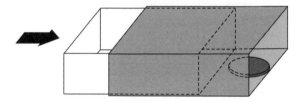

1 Slide out the drawer of the matchbox with the left hand. Hold the outside of the cover with the right hand, palm up.

2

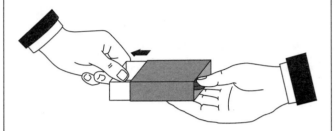

2 As the drawer slides out, move your right thumb inside the cover on top of the concealed coin (illustration 2).

3 Pull the drawer out of the cover and show it is empty. Show the back of the cover by turning the right hand palm down, keeping the coin secretly held inside with the right thumb.

4 Slide the drawer back inside (illustration 3). Your right hand is still palm down and therefore the coin will be trapped between the top edge of the drawer and the top

TOP TIPS FOR TRICKSTERS

Be warned! When people discover you are a magician they may say, "If you're a magician produce some money then!" Now you can!

of the cover (illustration 4). While the drawer is open the coin will stay in this position, but when pushed shut the coin will be heard dropping into the drawer. Place the box with the open drawer on the center of the table.

5 Take the duplicate coin under the table with your right hand and tap it against the underside of the table. Show that your left hand is empty and lift up the matchbox from the table.

6 Under the table your right hand slides the coin into your sock!

7 The left hand brings the matchbox down on the table and at the same time pushes the drawer closed. The coin can be heard dropping inside the matchbox.

3

8 Bring out your right hand to show it is empty, and ask someone to open the box to prove that the coin really has arrived inside.

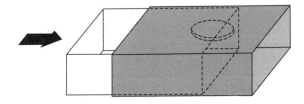

T. NELSON DOWNS (1867-1938)

T. Nelson Downs was an American magician who billed himself as the "King of Koins" (sic). As a railway clerk he spent his spare time learning sleight of hand with coins and creating his own variations. He turned professional and almost overnight became a big vaudeville star with his unique and original act of apparently producing coins from mid-air. One of his most challenging moves is the "Downs Coin Star" in which coins balanced on the tips of the four fingers and thumb vanish and re-appear.

GLASS THROUGH TABLE

Effect The magician covers a coin on the table with a glass. To conceal the coin the glass is covered with a napkin. The magician says that the coin is going to vanish. This doesn't happen, but when a spectator slaps down on the napkin-covered glass it squashes flat! The glass has penetrated through the table!

Requirements A smooth-sided drinking glass, two paper napkins and any coin (this could be borrowed).

Preparation For this effect to work you must be sitting at a table. Prepare by setting the props out in front of you on the table.

● ● ● ● ● ● ● ● ● ● ● ● ● ● ● ●

1

1 Explain to the audience that you are going to attempt to pass a solid object through the table top.

2 Place the coin on the table about 30cm/12in from the rear edge and cover it with the upturned glass, isolating the coin inside (illustration 1).

3 Open out the two napkins and lay them on top of each other covering the glass (illustration 2). Explain to the audience, "The coin must be covered to keep the secret!"

4 Pull the napkins down around the outside of the glass to show its outline and with one hand twist the glass tightly inside the napkins to show its shape more clearly (illustration 3).

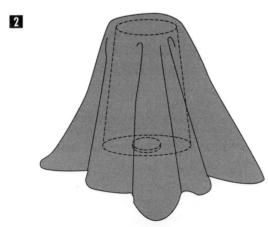

3

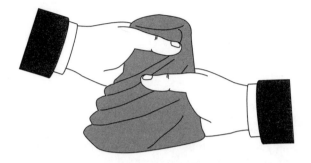

5 Lift the glass and napkins together to show the coin is still on the table. Replace the glass and napkins over the coin.

6 Ask everyone to concentrate on making the coin penetrate through the solid table. If you wish you can even get everyone to hold hands to form a "power circle"!

7 Lift up the glass and napkins together with the right hand and look suprised and disappointed that the coin is still there. Your left hand moves towards the coin to pick it up. While the audience's attention is on the coin, the right hand moves back to the edge of the table nearest you. The basic rule of misdirection is that wherever you look, the audience will look. It is important throughout the next few steps that you keep looking at the coin, not at your right hand.

8 Bring your right hand to rest on the edge of the table with the mouth of the glass pointing towards your lap.

9 Your left hand picks up the coin from the table to turn it over so that you can look at it more carefully to see what went wrong. At the same time your right fingers relax their grip on the glass through the napkin. The weight of the glass will make it slide out of the napkins into your waiting lap (illustration 4)! It is important that you lift your heels off the floor slightly to make your lap a "valley." This ensures the glass will roll into your lap and not on to the floor!

5

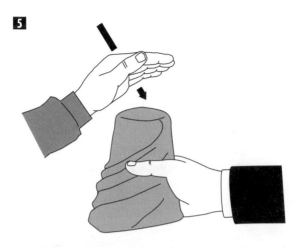

10 Hold the napkins gently in the right hand so that they keep the shape of the glass even though it is no longer there!

11 The left hand places the coin back in the center of the table and the right hand covers it with the napkins as though they still contained the glass. To the audience it should appear that nothing has changed – the big suprise is coming in a moment!

12 "It didn't work," you say, "because I forgot to get someone to tap the top of the glass." Ask a member of the audience to hold their hand just above the napkins (illustration 5). Try to get someone for this who you think will respond loudly to the surprise.

13 Hold your right hand above the spectator's hand and smash it down on the napkins (illustration 6). The napkins will squash flat and the spectator will usually scream!

14 Your right hand goes under the table and on the journey takes the glass from your lap. Lift up the napkins with your left hand to show that the coin is still there. Remove the right hand from under the table with the glass – to show that you did as you promised and passed a solid object right through the table!

6

TOP TIPS FOR TRICKSTERS

Even the most famous stage illusionists know a few small coin tricks that they can perform to maintain their reputation when off-stage!

FEATURE ITEMS

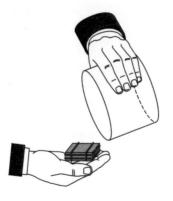

COIN IN THE BALL OF WOOL

Effect *This is in the miracle class, and when well rehearsed will make a great finale to any act or show you are putting on.*

A borrowed coin is marked. It vanishes while held by a member of the audience and appears inside a sealed matchbox which is wrapped in the centre of a ball of wool!

Requirements *A ball of heavy knitting wool, a regular sized matchbox, a large clear container (big enough to hold the ball of wool), four elastic bands, a special handkerchief and a special coin slide.*

Preparation *The handkerchief is made from any cotton handkerchief with a coin secretly sewn into one corner.*

1

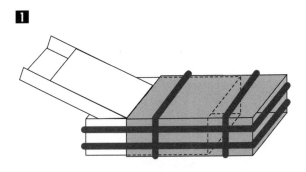

2

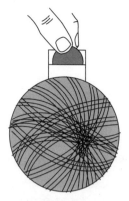

The coin slide is made from any piece of flat metal or cardboard. This is folded into a flat tube so that a coin can be dropped into one end and will slide down and out the other end. This is the secret prop for this effect.

Insert one end of the slide into the open drawer of the empty matchbox and wrap the four elastic bands around the matchbox as in illustration 1. The bands will hold the slide in position and close the box when the slide is removed.

Wrap the wool around the matchbox to form a ball with the matchbox hidden inside. Make sure the wool is not wrapped too tightly otherwise the slide may get stuck when you have to remove it at the crucial moment.

Place the prepared ball of wool out of sight on your table – inside a hat or large box is best.

1 Borrow a coin from a member of the audience and have them mark it with a pencil so they will recognize it in the future.

2 Wrap the marked coin in the special handkerchief. What really happens underneath the cover of the handkerchief is that you keep the borrowed coin finger-palmed in your right hand, and hand the secret sewn-in coin to a member of the audience to hold through the folds of the material. They will believe they are holding the borrowed coin wrapped inside the handkerchief.

3 Reach into your box (or wherever the ball of wool is) with your right hand and insert the marked coin in the coin slide (illustration 2). The coin will slide down into

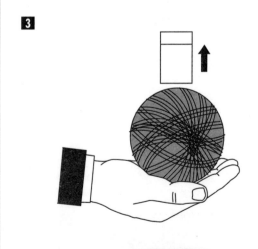

4

the matchbox wrapped inside the ball of wool. Pull the slide out of the ball of wool, leaving it in the box. Remove the ball of wool and put it in the clear container. Hand this to a spectator to hold.

4 Ask your "hanky holding helper" to stand up, and ask them if they are still holding on to the coin. After they have answered "yes" whip the handkerchief out of their hand and display it on both sides to show that the coin has vanished.

TOP TIPS FOR TRICKSTERS

The most important tip – which has been broken by every coin magician I know – is to be careful not to spend the fake coins you buy!

5 Ask the spectator holding the ball of wool to stand up and face the audience. Hand the end of the wool to the spectator who lent you the coin, and ask them to pull it (illustration 4). As they pull on the end, the ball of wool will twist and turn inside the container.

6 When the wool has all been unwound, the audience will see the matchbox inside the container. Ask another spectator to remove the box (illustration 5). Emphasize that at no point have you touched the box. Ask them to remove the rubber bands and open the box.

7 Inside the drawer is the actual marked coin that vanished moments before! Have the coin returned to its owner for verification and take your applause.

5

ADVANCED COIN AND BANKNOTE TRICKS

THE BASICS

COIN FOLD

Effect *The magician wraps a coin – which can be borrowed – securely in a sheet of paper. Despite the impossible conditions the coin vanishes.*

Requirements *A coin and a sheet of paper about 10 x 15cm/4 x 6in.*

Preparation *None.*

● ● ● ● ● ● ● ● ● ● ● ● ● ● ●

1 If the coin is borrowed from a member of the audience – and the effect is much stronger if it is – have them make a mark on the coin with a marker pen, so that they will recognize it.

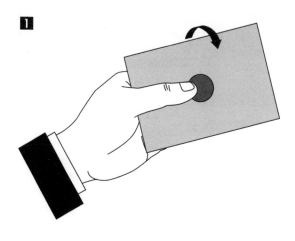

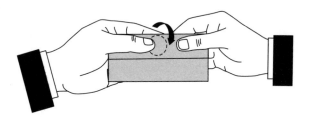

2 Place the coin in the center of the sheet of paper and hold it in your left hand as shown in illustration 1.

3 Your right hand folds the upper half of the paper over the coin (illustration 2). The coin is now hidden from you and the audience by the folded paper.

4 Fold the paper to the left of the coin away from you (illustration 3) to the back of the coin. This seals the coin inside the paper on the left edge.

5 Do the same with the paper on the right of the coin, folding it away from you to the back of the coin. This fold will overlap the fold you have just made from the left side. The coin is now trapped inside the packet from the left and right sides and from above. The bottom edge is still open. As you make the folds it is important the coin does not slide out (this would give the game away!) so maintain enough pressure on the coin to keep it inside.

6 The last fold is the special one! If you were to fold the paper below the coin towards you the coin would trapped inside – so you don't! The last fold is made upward but towards the audience, as the left and right folds were (illustration 4). This leaves the bottom edge of the packet open – and this is where the coin will make its exit.

7 Press the paper firmly around the coin to make an impression of the coin on the paper. This will "prove" to the audience that the coin is still there after it has gone from the packet.

3

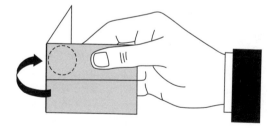

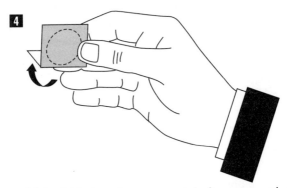

8 Hold the folded packet at your right fingertips with the secret opening at the bottom. Tap the packet on the table so that the audience can hear the coin inside. As your hand moves up from the table top, release your pressure on the coin inside and allow it to slide secretly into your right hand (illustration 5). This is a basic example of a magician's misdirection – the larger action of your hand moving up from the table will cover any small movement as the coin slides out of the packet.

9 You must now finger palm the coin (see Glossary). Don't worry about the audience seeing you do this. The fold is very convincing and the audience will not suspect that the coin can possibly escape, so you have no reason to worry about them spotting the coin. They are sure they know where it is! Simply hold the coin concealed in your curled fingers. If you look tense and worried *then* the audience will be suspicious!

10 Take the packet in your left hand and show the audience the impression of the coin in the paper. While the audience's attention is on the packet, you can secretly dispose of the coin hidden in your right hand in your right jacket or trouser pocket.

11 Bring the hands together and dramatically tear up the packet to show that despite the tight secure wrapping the coin has completely vanished!

12 You can now produce the coin from your pocket if you wish. Or you can consider it a profit and make a fast exit!

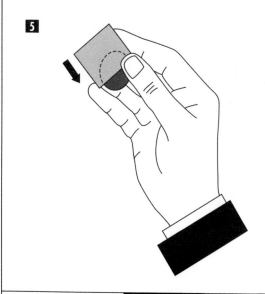

INTO THIN AIR

Effect *A coin vanishes from inside a matchbox.*

Requirements *A small coin and a specially prepared matchbox (see "Preparation").*

Preparation *Using a razor blade or sharp knife you cut a secret flap at the bottom of one end of the matchbox drawer. Cut along the thick lines shown on illustration 2 and lightly score inside the box along the dotted line. This will create a secret flap which will open unnoticed.*

• • • • • • • • • • • • • • • •

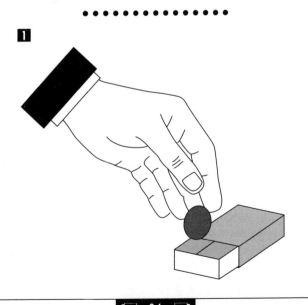

2

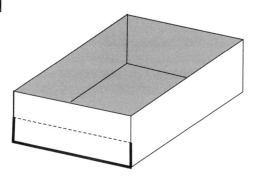

1 Push open the drawer so that the flap end remains hidden inside the cover.

2 Ask a spectator to drop the coin inside and push the drawer closed (illustration 1).

3 Pick up the box from the table and rattle it to prove the coin is inside.

ROSS BERTRAM (1912-1992)

Ross Bertram was considered by magicians to be the true heir to the throne of T. Nelson Downs – the new "King Of Koins". He was born in Toronto, Canada. He made his first big impact upon the world of magic when he appeared at magic conventions in the USA during the 1940s.

3

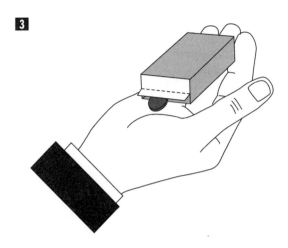

4 When you have finished rattling allow the coin to fall through the flap into your hand where you finger palm it (illustration 3).

5 Place the (now empty) matchbox on the table and secretly pocket the coin. You can now open the matchbox to show that the coin has vanished "into thin air"!

TOP TIPS FOR TRICKSTERS

Many different fake coins and coin "boxes" are available from magic shops and dealers. Some of these will be described in the following pages.

THE VANISHING BANKNOTE

Effect *A banknote vanishes inside the magician's hand.*

Requirements *A banknote.*

Preparation *The secret of this effect is the special fold which makes the banknote look like two. Prepare the note with this fold before the performance.*

Fold lines X–X and Y–Y away from you and lines A–A and B–B towards you (illustration 1). Fold the note along these creases so that it looks like illustration 2.

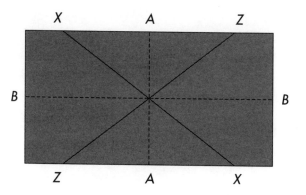

Now fold the point marked A to the right and the corresponding point B on the back to the right. It should now look as though you have two separate banknotes (illustration 3).

• • • • • • • • • • • • • • • •

1 Display the folded note in your right hand, telling the audience you have two notes.

2 Show your left hand empty and place the folded note inside. Say, "The two notes go into my empty hand."

3 Close your left hand into a fist.

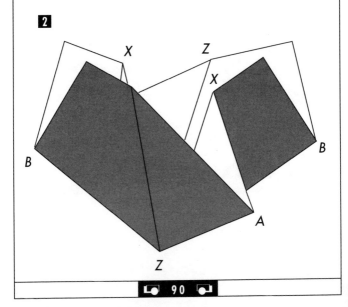

4 Reach into the top of your left fist with your right hand and remove the note, unfolding it as you do so. Say "We take one away, which leaves?"

5 After the audience have answered "one", open your hand to show that it is empty!

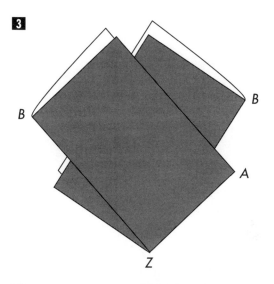

3

COIN TRICKS YOU CAN BUY

COIN UNIQUE This is a very effective set of fake coins with which you can make a coin vanish under apparently impossible conditions.

E-Z COIN VANISH

Effect *A marked coin vanishes from the magician's hand.*

Requirements *Any coin (the smaller the better), a pencil with an eraser on the end and a small piece of Blu-Tack.*

Preparation *Remove the eraser from the end of the pencil and stick the Blu-Tack inside the metal fitting that held it. Make sure plenty of Blu-Tack sticks out over the top of the fitting.*

• • • • • • • • • • • • • • •

1

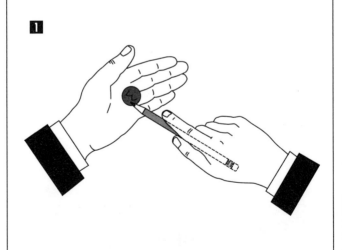

2

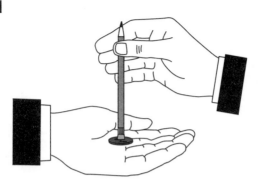

1 Hand someone the coin and the pencil and ask them to make a mark on the coin (illustration 1).

2 Take the coin and pencil back. Rest the coin mark side up on your open left hand. Hold the pencil between your right first finger and thumb. The Blu-Tack end of the pencil is hidden inside your hand.

TOP TIPS FOR TRICKSTERS

Always remember that the tricks that you do are just a peg for you to hang entertainment on. If you just fool people they will be puzzled – it is the situation you create that makes it entertaining.

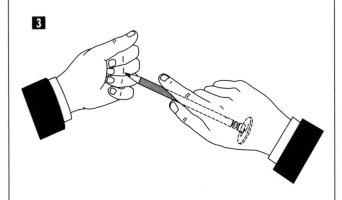

3 Bring your right hand over your left hand and tap the sticky end of the pencil on to the coin (illustration 2). Apparently you are indicating and referring to the mark made on the coin. Press hard so that the coin sticks to the end of the pencil.

4 Look at the audience to take attention away from your hands as you make some comment about the spectator's artistic ability. At this moment swing the end of the pencil – and the attached coin – into your right hand (illustration 3). At the same time close your left hand, as though it still contained the coin.

5 Tap on the back of the left hand with the pointed end of the pencil as though it were a magic wand. Place the pencil – and coin – in your pocket and open your left hand to show the coin has vanished!

TRANSPOSITION

TWO COINS

Effect *Two coins are covered with playing cards. Amazingly one coin vanishes and appears under the other card.*

Requirements *Two coins, two playing cards and a short length of thread. You will also need a good smooth surface to perform this effect.*

Preparation *Join the two coins together with the length of thread (illustration 1). The simplest way to do this is to tape an end of the thread to the bottom of each coin. The thread between the coins should be about 2.5cm/1in long. Place the prepared coins in your pocket along with your loose change.*

● ● ● ● ● ● ● ● ● ● ● ● ● ● ● ●

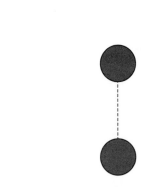

2

1 Remove a handful of change from your pocket and pick out the two prepared coins. Place them on the table (tape side down) as in illustration 1.

2 Cover the coin nearest you with a playing card (illustration 2).

3 Pick up the other playing card with your right hand, at the same time pushing the uncovered coin forward with your left hand.

4 As you do this, unknown to your audience, the covered coin will be pulled out from under the first card. This coin will be hidden by your left wrist (illustration 3).

5 The playing card in your right hand is dropped over the visible coin and covers the concealed coin at the same time.

6 Make a magical pass and then show that the coin has vanished from under the first card and both coins are now together under the second.

7 You can repeat this effect by using a different "steal" as follows. Begin with the coins side by side on the table. Cover the right coin with a card. With your left first finger push the visible coin until it is in position just next to the front short edge of the card. This "proves" to the audience that the coins are not connected.

8 The right hand uses the front short edge of the other card to slide the visible coin forward. Again, the second coin will be pulled along too, this time hidden below the moving card (illustration 4).

9 The right hand drops the card over both coins. Make a magical pass, and show the coin has passed again!

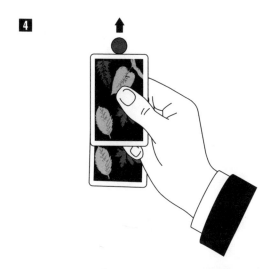

COIN TRICKS YOU CAN BUY

CIGARETTE THROUGH COIN   As its name suggests this is a special coin through which you can push a borrowed cigarette.

CLEVER STUFF

THE COIN ROLL

Effect *This is not a trick, but an impressive piece of digital dexterity to keep your hands supple and convince spectators of your ability with coins. It's not easy, but worth the effort.*

Requirements *Any coin.*

Preparation *None.*

• • • • • • • • • • • • • • • •

1 Clip the coin close to the edge by your right thumb and first finger so that it projects above the back of your hand (Illustration 1).

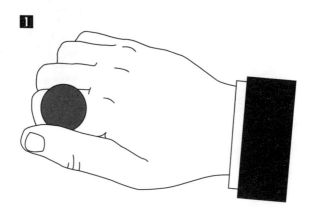

2 Push the coin up with your right thumb and release it, allowing it to roll over the back of your first finger near the knuckles and land between the first and second fingers (illustration 2).

3 Open the fingers to clip the coin between the first and second fingers.

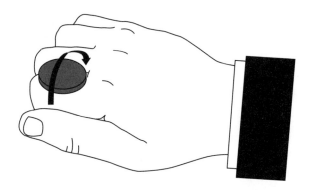

COIN TRICKS YOU CAN BUY

OKITO BOX   A specially machined brass box which can be used in many coin routines.

3

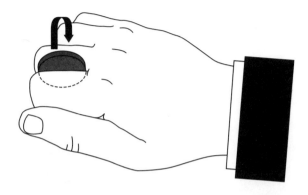

4 Raising the first finger, roll the coin into the gap between the second and third fingers, the third finger rising to clip the coin into position (illustration 3).

5 Move the coin into the final position (between the third and fourth fingers) by raising the second finger and rolling the coin over. Clip it with the fourth finger.

6 To move the coin back to the start, move your right thumb under the fourth finger. Slide the coin against the underside of the fingers, from its position clipped between the third and fourth fingers, until it is back between the thumb and first finger.

7 You are all set to repeat steps 1 to 6 again – and again. Until somebody watches!

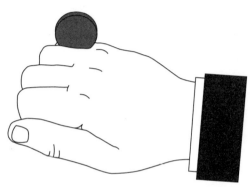

J.B. BOBO

J. B. Bobo is the author of Modern Coin Magic *which is every coin magician's bible. His family name was originally Beaubeaux, but was changed to Bobo when they emigrated to America. He was born in Texas, but spent his youth in Canada. After a career as a window display decorator he became a full-time magician and in 1952 wrote his classic book for which he is known by magicians around the world.*

THE ROLL DOWN

Effect *This is a mighty impressive flourish to do with four coins. This is not a trick – it is just a flashy display. Be warned that this is probably the most difficult effect in the book, but if you have the patience to learn it you will be able to do a piece of coin manipulation that will prove an effective display of your skills.*

Requirements *Four identical coins.*

Preparation *None.*

• • • • • • • • • • • • • • • •

1

1 Stack the four coins in a pile and hold them together between your right thumb and first finger. The hand should be palm up.

2 Bend your right second finger into the palm and tilt your hand very slightly to the left (illustration 1).

3 Release the thumb's pressure on the top two coins of the stack and, using the fourth finger, rotate them until they are wedged between the third and fourth fingers (illustration 2).

4 Lift your second finger and apply pressure with it to the edges of the top coin of each pair. Your thumb and fourth finger apply pressure to the edges of the lower coin of each pair.

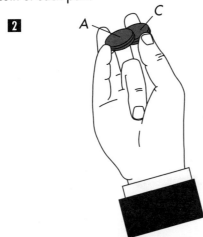

5 Slowly straighten out your fingers. Your thumb and fourth fingers pivot outwards splitting the two pairs of coins. The second finger rolls between the two centre coins holding their edges.

6 You now have a coin clipped between each finger.

BOBBY BERNARD

Bobby Bernard is British magic's best-known teacher, having produced many award-winning acts. He is also well known for his skill and innovative creations in the field of sleight of hand with coins. His stage act is a theatrical presentation of the magic of Isaac Fawkes, the well-known magician from the 1800s.

ADVANCED PRODUCTIONS

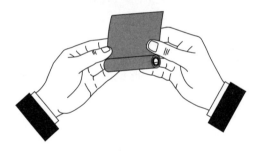

BANKNOTES FROM MID-AIR

Effect *This is an ideal opening to a stage or platform presentation. The magician comes on stage displaying empty hands, rolls up his sleeves and produces six genuine banknotes apparently from mid-air.*

Requirements *Six banknotes. You will also need to be wearing a jacket or sports coat.*

Preparation *Stack the banknotes into a pile and roll them into a very tight roll. Place the roll into the crook of your left elbow and pull the coat material over the top of the roll. The notes will stay rolled up if you keep your arm slightly bent (illustration 1).*

• • • • • • • • • • • • • • • •

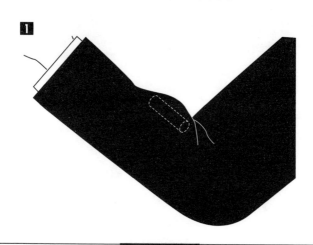

1 Walk on to the stage with the notes loaded as described. Show that your right hand is empty and with your left hand grab your jacket sleeve at the elbow and pull it up.

2 Show that your left hand is empty, and with your right hand grab your jacket sleeve at the elbow and pull it back. At the same time your right hand grabs the roll of notes which are hidden in the sleeve and keeps them concealed behind the right fingers (illustration 2).

3 Bring both hands together in front of you at shoulder height and, using the thumbs and fingers of both hands, unroll the notes (illustration 3).

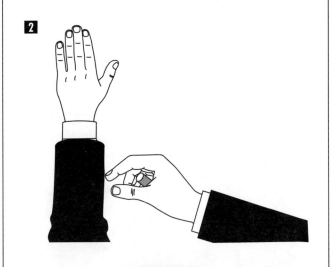

3

4 Unroll about half the length of the notes, and then slide your left hand down and unroll the bottom half with your left thumb. This leaves the open notes in your right hand where you can fan them out and take your applause.

KALANAG (1893-1963)

Kalanag was the stage name of Helmut Schreiber, a rotund German illusionist. After the Second World War he toured the world with his spectacular, colorful illusion show Sim Sala Bim (the same name as Dante's touring show). His show is now in the collection of the popular British magician, Paul Daniels. Almost as well known as Kalanag was his glamorous wife and number one assistant – Gloria.

DOUGH!

Effect *The magician breaks open a bun and finds a real coin inside! This trick is a particularly effective in a restaurant or buffet.*

Requirements *A small bun and a coin.*

Preparation *Secretly get a coin into your right hand where you hold it in finger palm position (see Glossary).*

• • • • • • • • • • • • • • •

1 Pick up the bun with your right hand, covering the coin hidden there.

2

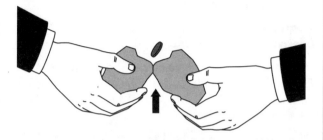

2 Your two hands bend the bun up first, making a small break underneath. Your right fingers secretly slip the coin into the break (illustration 1).

3 Both hands now bend the bun down to show the coin inside. It is important that you keep the two lower halves of the bun together during this stage (illustration 2).

4 You can now enjoy watching everybody break open their buns to see how much they have inside!

COIN TRICKS YOU CAN BUY

BOSTON BOX A special brass box, which is similar to the Okito Box, but capable of a lot more.

🪙 MAKING MONEY 🪙

Effect *The magician magically changes four blank pieces of paper into four genuine crisp banknotes!*

Requirements *Four identical banknotes, four blank banknote-sized pieces of paper and some glue.*

Preparation *Hold all the pieces of paper together. Fold in the right and left thirds, then fold the bottom third up and the top third down. Repeat this procedure with the four banknotes.*

Glue the two packages back to back. Then open out the blank sheets. Transfer the top white sheet to the bottom of the pile, covering the banknotes.

● ● ● ● ● ● ● ● ● ● ● ● ● ● ● ●

1

2

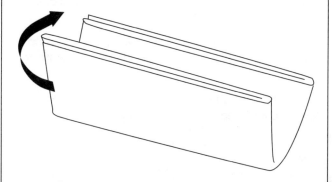

1 Hold the pile of papers in your left hand and show them front and back (illustration 1).

2 Your right hand removes the top sheet and shows it to be blank on both sides.

3 Follow the same procedure and show the second sheet blank both sides.

COIN TRICKS YOU CAN BUY

SHELL COIN   This special coin will enable you to perform "Coins Through the Table" or "Coins Across" with ease.

4 Do not show the third sheet – it has a bundle of banknotes stuck on the back!

5 Remove the bottom sheet and show both sides of it before replacing it back ON TOP of the pile.

6 The pile should be held so that everybody is looking down on it – so that the banknotes stuck underneath are concealed (illustration 3).

7 Fold the papers into a package along the creased lines you made earlier (illustration 2).

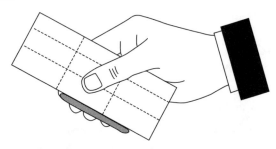

COIN TRICKS YOU CAN BUY

COPPER SANDWICH This is a more expensive gimmicked coin box which will enable you to perform more impressive effects.

8 Turn the package over (illustration 4) and open it to show that the blank paper has turned into banknotes. Move the top note to the bottom of the pile and repeat steps 1 to 5 to show they are genuine notes. Then fold them up and stick them in your wallet!

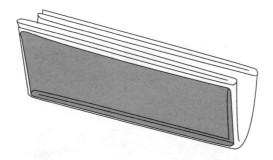

THE MAGIC CASTLE

The Magic Castle in Hollywood is considered by many to be the international home for magic. This large Victorian mansion up in the Hollywood hills (not far from the world famous sign) opened its doors as a private magic club in 1963. Only the many thousands of proud members and their guests are allowed to eat in the magical restaurant, watch the nightly magic shows and even see the Castle's piano playing ghost!

ADVANCED PENETRATIONS

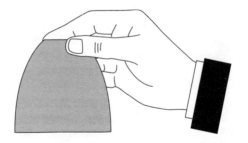

THROUGH THE HAND

Effect *A coin penetrates through the magician's hand.*

Requirements *Any coin.*

Preparation *None.*

• • • • • • • • • • • • • • • •

1 Show that your left hand is empty and close it into a fist. Turn it over so that the back of the hand is uppermost. Display the coin between the tips of the right fingers and thumb (illustration 1).

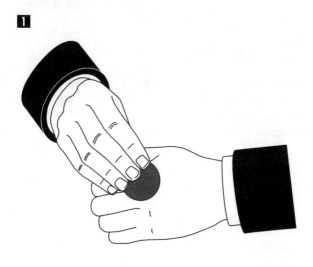

2 Press the coin against the back of the left hand as though trying to push it through. Slide the fingers of your right hand over the coin so that the coin is concealed from view (illustration 2).

3 Take the right hand away, keeping the coin concealed behind the fingers. Open your left hand and act surprised that the coin is not there.

COIN TRICKS YOU CAN BUY

DYNAMIC COINS   This makes a stack of coins appear and disappear from underneath brass caps.

4 As your left hand turns back to close into a fist again, your right fingers secretly allow the coin to fall into the left hand (illustration 3). Look at your audience while you are doing this, and they will look at you. This is a basic example of misdirection – controlling the audience's attention. The audience will also stop watching your hands if you relax, as though the trick has failed.

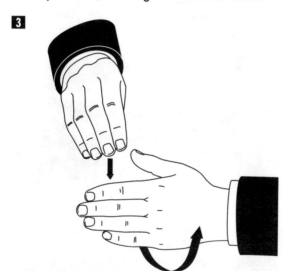

TOP TIPS FOR TRICKSTERS

The patter you use for your effects is just as important as the tricks – especially if it is part of the misdirection.

5 Say you will try it again. Rub the back of your left hand with the right fingers (illustration 4). Show that your right hand is now empty. Open your left hand to show the coin resting on your palm – having apparently passed through the back of your hand.

EMIL KIO (1900-1965)

Kio was a famous Russian illusionist who frequently performed with the Moscow State Circus. He baffled many magicians by performing illusions that are normally presented on stage – in the center of a circus ring, surrounded by the audience! After his death his son Igor followed in his footsteps.

PENCIL THROUGH NOTE

Effect *The magician wraps a banknote in a piece of paper and pierces the note and paper with a pencil. The magician shows the effect from all sides so that there is no doubt the pencil has punctured the note. The magician removes the pencil and allows a spectator to unfold the paper and note. Despite a hole in the center of the paper, the note is unharmed – demonstrating the strength of the currency!*

Requirements *A sheet of paper slightly bigger than a banknote, a banknote and a sharp pencil.*

Preparation *The banknote is prepared by cutting a slit near one of its short edges about 1cm/0.5in long (illustration 2). Put the note in your wallet with your regular money.*

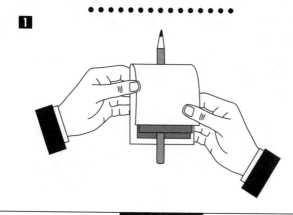

2

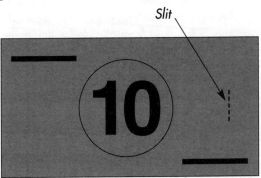

Slit

1 Remove the prepared note from your wallet. Show it to the audience, keeping your thumb over the slit.

2 Place the note on top of the paper, overlapping one end by about 0.5cm/0.25in (illustration 3).

3 Fold the note and paper towards you so that the note is sandwiched inside. Because the ends are not squared up, you have four steps of paper.

TOP TIPS FOR TRICKSTERS

If another magician shows you a trick don't ask, "How do you do that?" If they want to tell you, they will!

4 Insert the point of the pencil between the folds of the note (illustration 4). However, unknown to the audience, the pencil point passes through the secret slit and up behind the note. Illustration 5 shows you what really happens.

COIN TRICKS YOU CAN BUY

COIN WAND   This is a wand which catches coins from mid-air – but it is very rare nowadays.

4

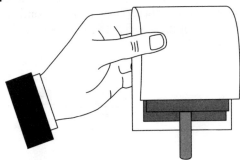

5 Continue pushing the end of the pencil until the point rips through the center of the paper (illustration 1). You can show the set-up on both sides so to the audience it really does seem that the pencil has torn through the center of the note.

6 Remove the pencil through the hole created in the paper. Unfold the paper and note, with the paper towards the audience. Separate your hands, holding the paper in one hand and the note in the other – to show the note is undamaged!

COIN TRICKS YOU CAN BUY

COIN TRAY A special tray that enables you to double your money with ease!

5

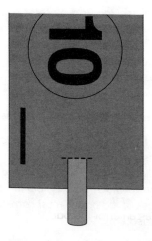

7 Replace the note in your wallet and try to remember not to spend it!

JASPER MASKELYNE (1902-1973)

Jasper was the youngest grandson of the famous J.N. Maskelyne (business partner of George Cooke and later David Devant). During the Second World War he was recruited to head a top secret "Magic Gang" of experts who used many stage illusion techniques to confuse the enemy. The story behind their adventures is detailed in David Fisher's book The War Magician.

🪙 HOLEY COIN FOLD 🪙

Effect *The magician shows a piece of paper which is punched with two holes – both too small for a coin to pass through. The magician demonstrates how it is possible to make a coin pass through a hole slightly smaller than the coin, but then goes on to visibly make the coin pass through a hole less than half its size!*

Requirements *Any large coin and a piece of paper.*

Preparation *Prepare the paper with folds and cut-outs as shown in illustration 1. The large hole A should be slightly smaller than the coin you intend to use. The small hole B can be much smaller, but the cut-outs around the edges of the paper must correspond when the paper is folded.*

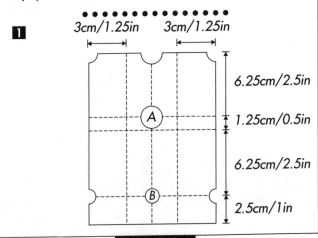

1 Display the paper and coin. Hold the coin against the large hole as in illustration 2. Fold the paper in half across the diameter of the hole.

2 Bend the sides of the paper inwards (illustration 3). The hole will widen and the coin will fall through without tearing the paper.

2

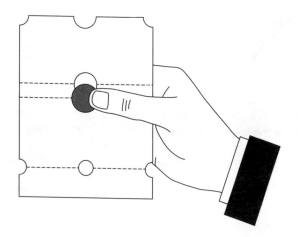

COIN TRICKS YOU CAN BUY

CASINO COIN   This enables you to change casino chips magically into real currency.

3

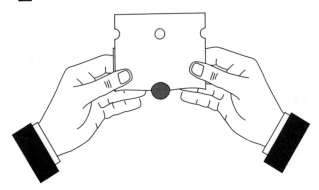

3 Now say that you will attempt the far more difficult task of making the coin pass through the smaller hole. Hold the coin in position just below the large hole (illustration 4). Fold the upper part of the paper down towards you over the coin. Fold the right and left sides away from you, making a package around the coin. Fold the bottom section up, away from you (illustration 5). It looks as if you have wrapped the coin securely, but actually the package is open at the bottom.

TOP TIPS FOR TRICKSTERS

You can always learn from watching other performers – not just magicians. Watch how they treat their audience and how the audience reacts to them.

4

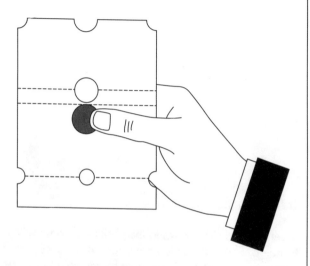

4 Keep a tight hold on the coin through the paper to prevent it slipping out prematurely through the secret opening. You are now going to complete the effect, performing it as a penetration.

TOP TIPS FOR TRICKSTERS

Even though money magic is easy to do at any time it does not mean you should do it all the time. Do not hog the limelight! Wait for people to ask to see a trick.

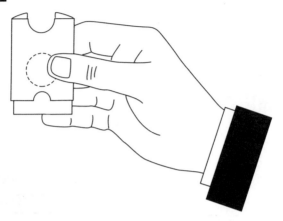

5 Let the coin slide down to the position shown in illustration 6. Show the folded paper on all sides, apparently proving that it is impossible for the coin to escape.

BUATIER DE KOLTA (1847-1903)

This French-born magician was probably the most creative and inventive magician of the 1800s. He invented the "Vanishing Birdcage" (made famous by Carl Hertz), the "Vanish of a Lady" while sitting in a chair, the production of flowers from an empty paper cone and "The Expanding Die", in which a small die grew larger until a woman climbed out of it!

6 Grasp the coin (apparently through the hole) and pull it free. Unfold the paper by reversing the process described in step 3 and show that it is completely undamaged!

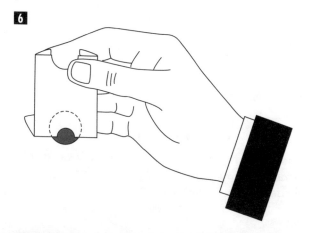

ALI BONGO

Although probably best known to the public for his work as a magic consultant for David Nixon and Paul Daniels, this Indian-born professional magician also performs in his own manic fast-paced act as the cartoon style "Shriek of Araby." His slick presentations of the "Knife Through Balloon" and the classic "Zombie Floating Ball" are admired by the magical fraternity around the world.

🪙 COIN THROUGH TABLE 🪙

Effect *Four coins are stacked in a pile on the table and covered with an upturned cup to prevent them escaping (illustration 1). Despite the tough security one coin does vanish and passes through the table top.*

Requirements *Four coins of identical value, an opaque cup and a cloth-covered table top.*

Preparation *There is no special preparation, but it is essential for this effect that you are sitting down at the table.*

• • • • • • • • • • • • • • • •

1 Stack the four coins in a pile near the back edge of the table top, with each coin slightly overlapping the coin below it as in illustration 2.

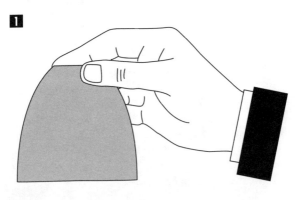

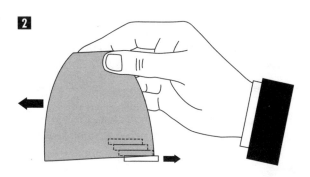

2 Cover the coins with the cup, ensuring that the back edge of the cup rests on top of the bottom coin of the stack as shown in illustration 2.

3 Slide the cup forward with the coins inside to a point nearer the center of the table. As you do this the cup will slide over the bottom coin, leaving it in its position on the table top. This coin will be concealed from the audience by your right arm.

4 Your right hand leaves the cup in the center of the table and slides back, pulling the hidden coin with it, until the coin falls into your lap (illustration 3).

TOP TIPS FOR TRICKSTERS

A good way to practice your patter (the words you say during your performance) is to record it with a tape recorder and then listen to it.

5 Show that your left hand is empty and place it under the table. Grab the coin from your lap with the left hand and hold it under the table. Tap the coin against the underside of the table top.

6 Ask a member of the audience to lift up the cup to show there are now only three coins. Bring the left hand out from under the table and throw the fourth coin on to the table top. It has apparently penetrated the table!

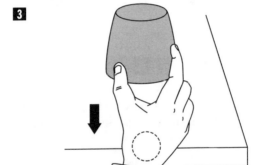

TOP TIPS FOR TRICKSTERS

Try to get out of the habit of asking your close family and friends for advice – they will either be too kind or too critical.

COIN THROUGH HANKY TWO

Effect The magician drapes a handkerchief over a borrowed coin. Magically the coin penetrates through the center of the handkerchief.

Requirements Any coin and a large cotton handkerchief. The effect is much stronger if both objects are borrowed from members of the audience, but it is advisable to have your own coin and handkerchief ready just in case nobody has a clean handkerchief or trusts you with their money!

• • • • • • • • • • • • • • • •

1

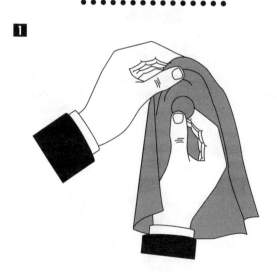

2

1 Display the coin at the tips of your right thumb and fingers. If you got a spectator to make a mark on the coin with a pen (which makes the effect much stronger) you can comment on their artistic ability – or lack of it!

2 Pick up the handkerchief with your left hand and holding it by the edge – not the corner – drape it over the coin and the right hand (illustration 1).

TOP TIPS FOR TRICKSTERS

Don't be afraid to ask members of the audience for constructive criticism after one of your performances. Hearing their comments will help you to improve.

3 Ensure that the front edge of the handkerchief (the one nearest the spectators) hangs lower down than the back edge (illustration 2).

4 Your left hand grips the coin through the material, from above, holding it between the thumb and fingers (illustration 3).

TOP TIPS FOR TRICKSTERS

Often a "lay person" (someone who does not know anything about magic) will be able to give constructive advice that another magician wouldn't think of.

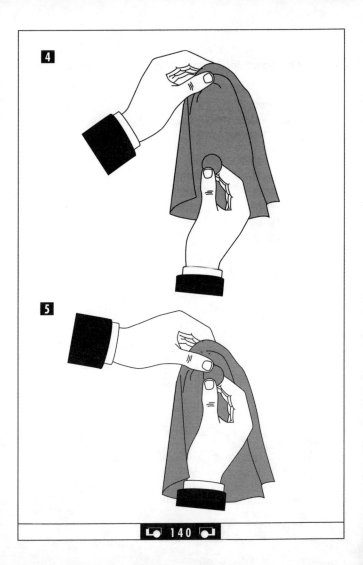

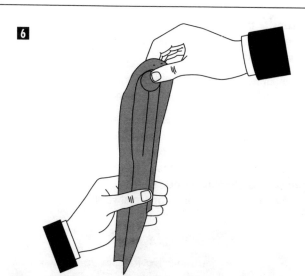

5 Now you remove your right hand from under the handkerchief – and secretly take the coin with it! Your right hand moves down, still holding on to the coin, below the rear edge of the handkerchief. This will not be seen by your audience because the front edge of the handkerchief is lower. Your left hand continues to hold the handkerchief at the center as though it were still holding the coin through the material!

6 Your right hand moves up behind the handkerchief with the coin remaining hidden (illustration 4). Slide the coin under your left thumb (illustration 5). Clip it between the thumb and the cloth.

7 Transfer the handkerchief and the clipped coin from the left hand to the right hand, ensuring that the coin remains hidden.

8 The left hand slides down the handkerchief and gathers all four corners tightly together (illustration 6).

9 The left hand jerks the handkerchief downwards out of your right hand, leaving the coin held at your right fingertips. It seems that the coin has visibly penetrated the center of the handkerchief! The coin and handkerchief can be examined and returned to their owners to prove that some magicians are trustworthy!

DAVID COPPERFIELD

The American illusionist David Copperfield is well known for his own television specials and spectacular stunts. In just over a decade he has vanished a Lear Jet, the Statue of Liberty and a coach from the Orient Express! He has walked through the Great Wall of China, vanished in the Bermuda Triangle and survived going over Niagara Falls!

He began by performing at children's parties as the "Great Davino" and appeared on his first TV show soon after playing the starring role in the musical The Magic Man. *He tours around the world with his live pop concert style show, during which he has been known to fly on stage or make the arena fill with snow!*

FEATURE EFFECTS

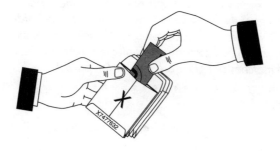

🎩 BURNT AND RESTORED NOTE 🎩

Effect *A borrowed banknote is burnt and reappears inside a sealed nest of boxes.*

Requirements *A banknote, an envelope, several boxes which fit inside each other, a pencil, scissors, an ashtray and a lighter or matches.*

Preparation *Cut a slit about 4cm/1.5in long halfway down the address side of the envelope (illustration 1). It is essential that the slit cannot be seen from the other side – even when the flap is open. Write the serial number of the banknote lightly in pencil on the inside of the flap. Fold the banknote up and place it inside the smallest of the boxes and nest all the boxes together. The matches or lighter are in your left pocket.*

• • • • • • • • • • • • • • • •

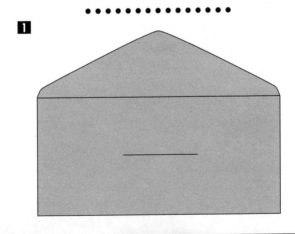

1

1 Ask for the loan of a banknote. This should match your note loaded inside the boxes.

2 Hand a member of the audience the nest of sealed boxes to guard.

3 Fold the borrowed banknote small enough to fit through the slit in the envelope. Place the note inside the envelope. Keep your left hand over the slit.

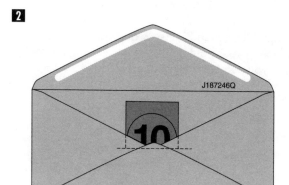

TOP TIPS FOR TRICKSTERS

If you want to put together an act to perform on stage it is good idea to get a local drama teacher or amateur director to help you "produce" it.

4 Now you suddenly "remember" that no one has taken a note of the serial number. Remove the note, unfold it and pretend to read the serial number – in fact you read the number on the flap. Of course this is the number of the note sealed inside the boxes! Ask the audience to remember the number.

5 Fold the note and put it back inside the envelope, but this time you push it partly through the slit in the address side (illustration 2). Again make sure this is covered by your left hand. Show that the note is really inside the envelope (illustration 3), then seal it up. Take the envelope in your right hand, secretly leaving the folded note in your left hand (illustration 4).

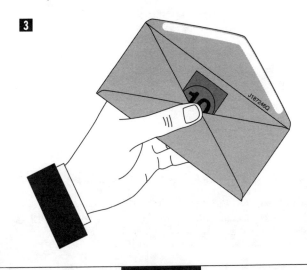

4

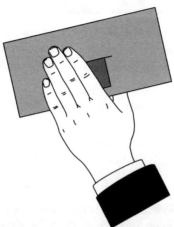

6 Put your left hand in your pocket to remove the matches or lighter, and leave the note in the pocket.

7 Set light to the envelope, explaining that there are new indestructible banknotes and you think this one of them. Drop the burning envelope into the ashtray where it quickly becomes apparent that this isn't one of those notes!

8 After the envelope has burnt completely ask the spectator holding the nest of boxes to join you. Ask them to open the first box. Inside is another box. Ask them to open that . . . and so on until all the boxes have been opened. Inside the last box is a banknote – when the serial number is read out, it is the same as the number of the banknote that has just burnt!

FLYING COIN

Effect *A coin is placed in a glass and covered with a handkerchief. At the magician's command the coin leaves the glass and appears in the center of a ball of wool!*

Requirements *Two duplicate coins, a glass, a handkerchief, an elastic band and a ball of wool.*

Preparation *Place one of the coins in the center of the ball of wool. Have the ball of wool near at hand.*

• • • • • • • • • • • • • • • •

1 Drop the coin into the glass and cover the mouth of the glass with the handkerchief. Place the elastic band over the mouth of the glass to hold the handkerchief in position. The elastic band should be around the middle of the glass, and not too tight (illustration 1).

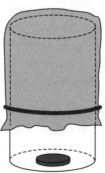

2

2 Pick up the glass with the left hand, sliding the handkerchief and the elastic band up about 2.5cm/1in to give you some slack in the top of the handkerchief (illustration 2).

3 Shake the glass so that the coin can be heard by the audience rattling inside. Tip the mouth of the glass towards the right hand. When you hear the coin make a clinking sound, close the right hand into a fist as though the coin had been tipped into it (illustration 3).

TOP TIPS FOR TRICKSTERS

If you do become a famous magician and get to see your name in lights, I hope you'll find the time to write to me and say "Thank you"!

4 Replace the glass on the table. Because of the slack, the coin is now trapped in a fold of the handkerchief and is hanging outside the mouth of the glass (illustration 4). (When you place the glass on the table make sure the secret fold is hanging at the back of the glass.) The audience can see through the glass – it is empty!

5 Make a tossing motion towards the ball of wool with the right hand. Show that the right hand is empty. Show that the left hand is empty. Take hold of the fold of handkerchief with the right hand, clipping the coin through the material. Pull the handkerchief off the glass leaving the elastic band behind. Place the handkerchief in your pocket along with the coin.

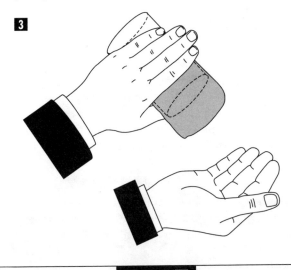

6 The coin has vanished! Hand a member of the audience the ball of wool and ask them to unravel it. Inside is the coin!

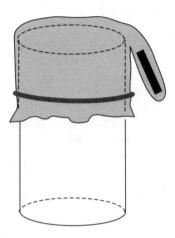

ORSON WELLS (1915-1985)

The "boy wonder" director, writer and author, famed for the radio version of War of the Worlds *and the movie masterpiece* Citizen Kane *was also an enthusiastic amateur magician. He frequently included magic in his films and shows, and in 1943 he staged and starred in his own magic show –* The Mercury Wonder Show *– in a big top in Hollywood. His assistant for the show was the young Marlene Dietrich.*

THE BILL IN LEMON

Effect *A borrowed banknote changes into an I.O.U. The note is found inside a lemon which a member of the audience was holding before the note was borrowed!*

This requires a lengthy set-up, but it is worth it for the memorable effect that it has. This is a true "classic" of magic.

Requirements *A stack of small pay envelopes, a lemon, a banknote, a handwritten I.O.U. the same size as the note, an elastic band, a knife, a pencil, glue and a small transparent plastic bag.*

Preparation *To prepare the envelopes, first write the serial number of your note near the bottom edge of one of the envelopes, as in illustration 3 (the envelope has*

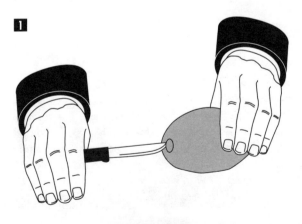

2

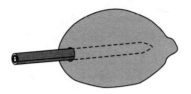

been marked with an "O" simply to identify it). Fold the I.O.U. and place it inside this envelope. Carefully cut the flap off one of the other envelopes (which has been marked with an X in the illustrations). Place envelope O on top of the stack of envelopes (serial number upwards) and place envelope X directly on top (illustration 4). Wrap the elastic band around all the envelopes. If done correctly it should appear that the gummed flap of envelope O belongs to the flapless envelope X.

To prepare the lemon, carefully cut around the point where the stalk was attached using the tip of a knife (illustration 1). Now make a larger hole inside the lemon by pushing a small round stick into the hole – this will make the necessary space for the banknote. It is important you do not puncture the juicy sections of the lemon or push too far and pierce the skin at the other end.

Roll the note into a tight compact roll and push it completely inside the hole you have just made in the lemon (illustration 2). Glue the section you removed back in place to cover the hole.

Place the lemon inside the plastic bag and place it on your table alongside the prepared stack of envelopes, the knife and pencil.

• • • • • • • • • • • • • • • •

1 Hand a member of the audience the lemon inside the bag and get them to hold it up high so that everybody can see it.

2 From the audience borrow a banknote to match your note in the lemon.

3 Pick up the stack of envelopes and pencil, and copy the number from their note on the bottom of envelope X.

3

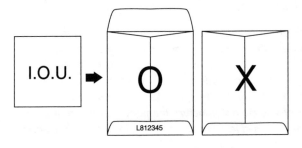

4

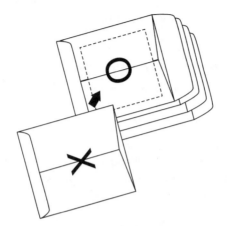

4 Fold the note into quarters and push it inside the flapless envelope X (illustration 5). Show the audience that the note is really going inside the envelope. Turn all the envelopes over and pull up on the flap sticking out. This will pull envelope O out of the stack, and envelope X with the note inside – and the real serial number written on it – will be kept in place on the bottom of the stack by the elastic band.

COIN TRICKS YOU CAN BUY

FOLDING COIN   This is a special coin which will enable you to push a large coin inside a bottle and do many other impressive tricks.

5 Dump the stack of envelopes face down on your table (illustration 7) and seal up envelope O. Hand it to someone in the audience to hold. Because it has a serial number written on it the audience will be convinced it is the same envelope they saw the note go into!

6 Ask the spectator to hold up the envelope to the light to check they can see the outline of the note. They say they can, because they see the outline of the I.O.U.!

7 Make a magical pass and ask them to open the envelope. Inside they will find your I.O.U. Tell them to hang on to it – and the envelope as that bears the serial number.

5

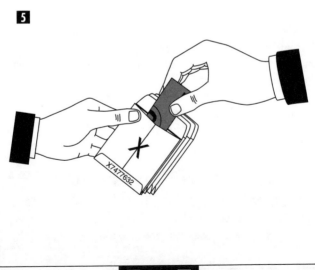

6

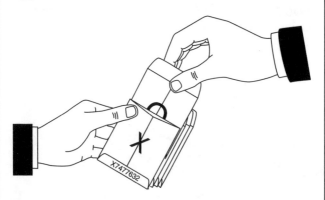

8 Invite the spectator who has been holding the bag throughout the trick up to assist you. Ask them to confirm that they were holding the lemon even before a note was borrowed. Get them to remove the lemon, then hand them the knife and ask them to cut it open.

9 When they pull the two halves apart they will find inside the lemon they have been holding from the very

TOP TIPS FOR TRICKSTERS

The most important rule of all is to make sure that before you go on stage you always check your flies are done up!

beginning – a banknote. Ask them to read out the serial number – it matches exactly the one on the envelope. Swap the note for the I.O.U. and enjoy the tremendous applause which will come your way!

7

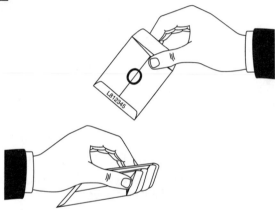

JOHN CALVERT

This former American film star travelled the world with his spectacular illusion show Magicarama. One of the highlights was to make a large musical organ float off the stage up over the footlights and beyond the orchestra pit.

INDEX

A
Advanced tricks
 basics, 80-94
 clever stuff, 100-107
 penetrations, 118-142
 productions, 108-117
 transposition, 95-99
Alternative Appearance, 44-46

B
Banknotes From Mid-Air, 109-111
Bernard, Bobby, 107
Bertram, Ross, 87
The Bill In Lemon, 152-158
Bobo, J.B., 104
Bongo, Ali, 133
Burnt And Restored Note, 144-147

C
Calvert, John, 158
Clever tricks
The Coin Roll, 101-104
The Roll Down, 105-107
Coin Escape, 54-55
Coin Fold, 81-85
Coin In The Ball of Wool, 74-78
The Coin Roll, 101-104
Coin Through Hanky Two, 137-142
Coin Through Leg, 51-53
Coin Through Table, 134-136
Coin Up Through Hand, 48-50
Continuous Coins, 33-38
Copperfield, David, 142
Crash Glass, 60-62

D
Daniels, Paul, 27
De Kolta, Buatier, 132
Dough!, 112-113
Downs, T. Nelson, 66

E
E-Z Coin Vanish, 92-94

F
Feature effects, 143-158
 The Bill In Lemon, 152-158
 Burnt And Restored Note, 144-147
 Flying Coin, 148-151
Feature items, 73-78
The Finger Palm, 14-16
Flying Coin, 148-151
The French Drop, 17-19

G
Glass Through Table, 67-72
Goshman, Al, 46

H
Hoffmann, Professor, 50
Holey Coin Fold, 128-133

I
Into Thin Air, 86-88

J
Jumping Coin, 5-6

K
Kalanag, 111
Kaps, Fred, 28
"King of Koins," 66, 87

M
The Magic Castle, 117
Making Money, 114-117
Maskelyne, Jasper, 127
Miser's Dream, 39-43
Money Making Machine, 25-28
Multiply Your Money, 29-32
Mystery Of The Sealed Box, 63-66

P

Pencil Through Note, 123-127
Penetrating Note, 56-59
Penetrations
 advanced
  Coin Through Hanky Two, 137-142
  Coin Through Table, 134-136
  Holey Coin Fold, 128-133
  Pencil Through Note, 123-127
  Through The Hand, 119-122
 basic
  Coin Escape, 54-55
  Coin Through Leg, 51-53
  Coin Up Through Hand, 48-50
  Crash Glass, 60-62
  Glass Through Table, 67-72
  Mystery Of The Sealed Box, 63-66
Penetrating Note, 56-59
Penn and Teller, 62
The Pinch Vanish, 20-23
Productions, 24-46
 advanced
  Banknotes From Mid-Air, 109-111
  Dough!, 112-113
  Making Money, 114-117
 basic
  Alternative Appearance, 44-46
  Continuous Coins, 33-38
  Miser's Dream, 39-43
  Money Making Machine, 25-28
  Multiply Your Money, 29-32

R

Reflex Tester, 7-9
The Roll Down, 105-107
Roth, David, 21

S

Simple tricks, 4-12
 Jumping Coin, 5-6
 Reflex Tester, 7-9
 Vanishing Note, 10-12
Sleight-of-hand vanishes. See Vanishes
Soo, Chung Ling, 23
Street magicians, 43

T

Through The Hand, 119-122
Tips for tricksters. See under specific tricks
Transposition, 96-99
Two Coins, 96-99

V

Vanishes
 E-Z Coin, 92-94
 The Finger Palm, 14-16
 The French Drop, 17-19
 The Pinch, 20-23
The Vanishing Banknote, 89-91
Vanishing Note, 10-12

W

Wells, Orson, 151